Air Fryer Cookbook for Beginners 2021

Your Everyday Air Fryer Book for Easy and Tasty Recipes to Fry Delicious Fish

Joann K. Conrad

By reading this document, the reader agrees that under no circumstances is the author responsible for any losses, direct or indirect, which are incurred as a result of the use of information contained within this document, including, but not limited to, — errors, omissions, or inaccuracies.

Table of Contents

INTRODUCTION............7

How Do Air Fryers Work? .7

Air Fryer Benefits...............8

Is an Air Fryer Useful in my Life?
..........................8

Using an Air Fryer Mean: ..8

• Cooking multiple dishes simultaneously........8

How Should I Clean my Air Fryer? 8

FISH.............................. 11

Tilapia Bites 12

Tuna Sandwich with Mozzarella and Mayonnaise 14

Broiled Tilapia Fillets 16

White Fish Fillets with Greek Yougurt..18

Panko White Fish Nuggets 20

Fish en Papillote with Herbs 22

Barramundi Fillets 24

Fish and Chips 26

Mediterranean Salmon with Asparagus 28

Cod Nuggets with Avocado 30

Cod Fillets with Soy Sauce.........32

Cod Pesto Sandwich 34

Fish Finger Sticks 36

Crispy Haddock Cake 38

Seafood Casserole with Cheddar Cheese and Red Chili.................40

Creole Trout Fillets 42

Salmon Fillets 44

Salmon with Greek Sauce 46

Tuna Patties...................................48

French Trout a la Meunière.......50

Fried Catfish.................................52

Cod Fillets.....................................54

Black Cod with Fennel and Pecans..56

Spicy Sardine Cake 58

White Fish Fillets with Romano Cheese..60

Jamaican Hoki Fillets 62

Kimchi Salmon 64

"Blackened" Catfish.....................66

Oaty Salmon and Haddock Fishcake...68

Parmesan Cheese Fillets.............70

Corn Tortillas with Halibut Fillets
....72

Lemon Pepper Haddock.............74

Pistachio Crusted Salmon 76

Marinated Tuna with Red Pepper Flakes...78

Cod Fingers 80

Catfish Fillets................................82

Salmon and Onion Balls 84

Salmon Cake with Fresh Parsley
....86

Salmon Croquettes with mayonnaise 88

Salmon Fillets with Broccoli......90

Salmon Tarts 91

Halibut Fillets with crumbled biscuits........**Errore. Il segnalibro non è definito.**

Smoked Fish Balls with Grana

Padano Cheese .... **Errore. Il segnalibro non è definito.**
Smoked Fish Quiche ..... **Errore. Il segnalibro non è definito.**
Smoked Salmon and Cheddar Taquitos ..... **Errore. Il segnalibro non è definito.**
Smoked Trout Frittata .. **Errore. Il segnalibro non è definito.**
Cod Fillets with Soy Sauce **Errore. Il segnalibro non è definito.**
Caribbean Salmon Fillets .. **Errore. Il segnalibro non è definito.**
Crispy Salmon .... **Errore. Il segnalibro non è definito.**
Alaskan Salmon Fillets .. **Errore. Il segnalibro non è definito.**

MEASUREMENT CONVERSIONS 93

WEIGHT EQUIVALENTS 94
VOLUME EQUIVALENTS (DRY) 94
VOLUME EQUIVALENTS (LIQUID) 95
AIR FRYER TEMPERATURES 96

AIR FRYER COOKING CHART 97

CREDITS 98

INTRODUCTION

Welcome to my air fryer cookbook.

Here you will learn how to cook delicious and healthy food while saving money and keeping the line. Yes, it's all true! That's what happen when you learn how to air fry your favorite meals. And it does not matter if you are a very beginner chef or not, my recipes are suitable for all air fryer models and no cooking experience is required, just a bit of love for tasty food.

How Do Air Fryers Work?

Let's say that air fryers work like amazing convection ovens. They are small ovens, yet mighty, and you can roast, broil, or bake in them.

Do you need to refresh how convection ovens work? No problem.

As heat rises, in a conventional oven the top rack is always the hottest spot, which leads to uneven doneness. (That's why no cookie recipe is good enough if you forget to rotate baking sheets from top to bottom and back to front midway through baking.)

In modern convection ovens, a couple of fans blow hot air around, and they equalize the temperature throughout the oven. Thanks to a similar air flow system, air fryers ensure a perfect heat distribution; then they preserve the right temperature in all sides of your food like only hot oil could do.

Air Fryer Benefits

Is your favorite dish french fries, grilled potatoes, muffins or chicken tenders? Well, you can prepare it all in an air fryer, with benefits that only an air fryer can offer:

- Low-fat diets
- Healthy meals
- Easy clean-up systems
- Meals can be perfectly cooked
- Oils and fats are not needed
- No unwanted aroma of fried foods invades your home

Is an Air Fryer Useful in my Life?

If you expect to fry, grill, bake, or roast your meals, an air fryer can pretty much do it all, and you will love it.

Using an Air Fryer Mean:

- Cooking multiple dishes simultaneously
- Cutting back on saturated fats
- Preparing healthy food within minutes
- Cooking your meal with hot air but preserving the same great look and taste as oiled fried foods.
- Avoiding those greasy stains on your plates, clothes and fingers.
- Adding minimum quantities of oil and only if you want to.

How Should I Clean my Air Fryer?

Definitely, you do not need to fret after using your air fryer. The most popular models were designed for hassle-free cleaning. Only non-stick materials were used, this prevents any food from sticking to surfaces that ultimately would make it hard to clean. Not less important, when your ingredients are cooked to perfection, you do not need to brush burnt surfaces, you can simply clean them in your dishwasher. Finally, all critical components such as the grill, pan and basket can be removed.

Once said that, just be sure to respect the basics:

- Use only suitable detergents
- For a maximum and quick cleaning, leave the pan to soak in hot water and detergent for a few minutes.
- Avoid using metal utensils when cleaning the appliance to prevent scuffs and scratches.
- For your safety, let the fryer cool off (30 minutes minimum) before you clean it.

I hope that you will enjoy my recipes, I am sure that you will create hundreds of healthy and tasty dishes!

FISH

Tilapia Bites

INGREDIENTS (4 Servings)

1 lb tilapia fillets, cut into chunks

½ cup cornflakes

1 cup flour

2 eggs, beaten

Salt to taste

Lemon wedges for serving

DIRECTIONS (Total Time: 25 minutes)

Preheat the fryer to 390 F. Pour the flour, eggs, and cornflakes each into 3 different bowls. Salt the fish and dip first in the flour, then in the eggs, and finally in the cornflakes. Put in the greased frying basket and AirFry for 6 minutes. Shake or flip, and cook for 5 more minutes or until crispy. Serve with lemon.

Tuna Sandwich with Mozzarella and Mayonnaise

INGREDIENTS (2 Servings)

4 white bread slices

1 (5-oz) can tuna, drained

½ onion, finely chopped

2 tbsp mayonnaise

1 cup mozzarella cheese, shredded

1 tbsp olive oil

DIRECTIONS (Total Time: 20 minutes)

In a small bowl, mix tuna, onion, and mayonnaise. Spoon the mixture over two bread slices, top with mozzarella cheese, and cover with the remaining bread slices. Brush with olive oil and arrange the sandwiches in the frying basket. Bake at 360 F for 7-10 minutes, flipping once halfway through. Serve.

Broiled Tilapia Fillets

INGREDIENTS (4 Servings)

1 lb tilapia fillets

1 tsp old bay seasoning

2 tbsp canola oil

2 tbsp lemon pepper

Salt to taste

2 butter buds

DIRECTIONS (Total Time: 20 minutes)

Turn on the air fryer and bring it to 400 F. Drizzle the fillets with canola oil. In a bowl, mix salt, lemon pepper, butter buds, and old bay seasoning; spread onto the fish. Place the fillets in the frying basket and AirFry for 10-12 minutes, turning once, until crispy. Serve with green salad.

White Fish Fillets with Greek Yougurt

INGREDIENTS (4 Servings)

4 lemon wedges

2 eggs

1 cup ale beer

1 cup flour

Salt and black pepper to taste

4 white fish fillets

½ cup light mayonnaise

½ cup Greek yogurt

2 dill pickles, chopped

1 tbsp capers

1 tbsp fresh dill, roughly chopped

Lemon wedges to serve

DIRECTIONS (Total Time: 25 minutes)

Turn on the air fryer and bring it to 390 F. Beat the eggs in a bowl along with the ale beer, salt, and pepper. Dredge the fillets in the flour and shake off the excess. Dip them into the egg mixture and then in the flour again. Spray with cooking spray and place in the frying basket. AirFry for 10-12 minutes, turning once. In a bowl, mix the mayonnaise, Greek yogurt, capers, salt, and dill pickles. Sprinkle the fish with a little bit of dill and serve with the sauce and some freshly cut lemon wedges on the side.

Panko White Fish Nuggets

INGREDIENTS   (4 Servings)

1 lb white fish fillets

1 lemon, juiced

Salt and black pepper to taste

1 tsp dried dill 4 tbsp mayonnaise

2 eggs, beaten

1 tbsp garlic powder

1 cup breadcrumbs

1 tsp paprika

DIRECTIONS (Total Time: 20 minutes)

Turn on the air fryer and bring it to 400 F. Season the fish with salt and black pepper. In a bowl, mix the beaten eggs, lemon juice, and mayonnaise. In a separate bowl, mix the crumbs, paprika, dill, and garlic. Dredge the fillets in the eggs and then in the crumbs. Place them in the greased frying basket and AirFry for 14-16 minutes, flipping once halfway through cooking. Serve with tomato chutney if desired.

Fish en Papillote with Herbs

INGREDIENTS (2 Servings)

2 whole trouts, scaled and cleaned

¼ bulb fennel, sliced

½ brown onion, sliced

1 tbsp fresh parsley, chopped

1 tbsp fresh dill, chopped

1 tbsp olive oil

1 lemon, sliced Garlic

salt and black pepper to taste

DIRECTIONS (Total Time: 25 minutes)

In a bowl, whisk the olive oil, brown onion, parsley, dill, fennel, garlic salt, and pepper. Turn on the air fryer and bring it to 350 F. Open the cavity of the fish and fill with the spicy mixture. Wrap the fish completely in parchment paper and then in foil. Place the fish in the frying basket and Bake for 15 minutes. Remove the foil and paper. Top with lemon slices and serve warm.

Barramundi Fillets

4 barramundi fillets

1 lemon, juiced

Salt and black pepper to taste

2 tbsp butter

½ cup white wine

8 black peppercorns

2 cloves garlic, minced

2 shallots, chopped

DIRECTIONS (Total Time: 30 minutes)

Turn on the air fryer and bring it to 390 F. Season the fillets with salt and black pepper. Place them in the greased frying basket. AirFry for 15 minutes, flipping once, until the edges are golden brown. Remove to a plate. Melt the butter in a pan over low heat. Add in garlic and shallots and stir-fry for 3 minutes. Pour in the white wine, lemon juice, and peppercorns. Cook until the liquid is reduced by three quarters, about 3-5 minutes. Adjust the seasoning and strain the sauce. Drizzle the sauce over the fish and serve warm.

FOTO 1

Fish and Chips

INGREDIENTS (4 Servings)

2 tbsp olive oil

4 potatoes, cut into thin slices

4 white fish fillets

1 cup flour

2 eggs, beaten

1 cup breadcrumbs

Salt and black pepper to taste

DIRECTIONS (Total Time: 30 minutes)

Turn on the air fryer and bring it to 400 F. Drizzle the potatoes with olive oil and season with salt and black pepper; toss to coat. Place them in the greased frying basket and AirFry for 10 minutes. Season the fillets with salt and black pepper. Coat them with flour, then dip in the eggs, and finally into the crumbs. Shake the potatoes and add in the fish; cook until the fish is crispy, 8-10 minutes. Serve.

Mediterranean Salmon with Asparagus

INGREDIENTS (2 Servings)

2 salmon fillets

Salt and black pepper to taste

1 lemon, cut into wedges

8 asparagus spears, trimmed

DIRECTIONS (Total Time: 20 minutes)

Turn on the air fryer and bring it to 350 F. Spritz the salmon with cooking spray. Season the fillets and asparagus with salt and pepper. Arrange the asparagus evenly in a single layer in the greased frying basket and top with the fillets. AirFry for 10-12 minutes at 350 F, turning the fish once. Serve with lemon wedges.

Cod Nuggets with Avocado

INGREDIENTS (4 Servings)

1 ¼ lb cod fillets, cut into

4 chunks each

½ cup flour

2 eggs, beaten

1 cup cornflakes

1 tbsp olive oil

Salt and black pepper to taste

1 avocado, chopped

1 lime, juiced

DIRECTIONS (Total Time: 25 minutes)

Mash the avocado with a fork in a small bowl. Stir in the lime juice and salt and set aside. Pour the olive oil and cornflakes in a food processor and process until crumbed. Season the fish with salt and pepper. Turn on the air fryer and bring it to 350 F. Place flour, eggs and cornflakes in 3 separate bowls. Coat the fish in flour, dip in the eggs, then coat in the cornflakes. AirFry in the greased frying basket for 14-16 minutes, shaking once or twice, until golden. Serve with the avocado dip.

Cod Fillets with Soy Sauce

INGREDIENTS (4 Servings)

1 lb cod fillets

2 tbsp fresh cilantro, chopped

Salt to taste

4 green onions, chopped

1 cup water

1 tbsp ginger paste

5 tbsp light soy sauce

2 tbsp olive oil

1 tsp soy sauce

2 cubes rock sugar

DIRECTIONS (Total Time: 20 minutes)

Turn on the air fryer and bring it to 360 F. Season the fillets with salt and drizzle with olive oil. Place in the frying basket and AirFry for 14-16 minutes, turning once. Meanwhile, heat the remaining oil in a pan over medium heat. Stir-fry the remaining ingredients for 5 minutes. Pour the sauce over the fish to serve.

Cod Pesto Sandwich

INGREDIENTS (4 Servings)

4 cod fillets

4 bread rolls

1 cup breadcrumbs

4 tbsp pesto sauce

4 lettuce leaves

Salt and black pepper to taste

DIRECTIONS (Total Time: 20 minutes)

Turn on the air fryer and bring it to 370 F. Season the fillets with salt and black pepper and coat them in breadcrumbs. Arrange them on the greased frying basket and Bake for 13-15 minutes, flipping once. Cut the bread rolls in half. Divide lettuce leaves between the bottom halves and place the fillets over. Spread the pesto sauce on top of the fillets and cover with the remaining halves. Serve warm.

Fish Finger Sticks

INGREDIENTS (4 Servings)

2 fresh white fish fillets, cut into

4 fingers each

1 egg

½ cup buttermilk

1 cup panko breadcrumbs

Salt and black pepper to taste

1 cup aioli (or garlic mayo)

DIRECTIONS (Total Time: 20 minutes)

Turn on the air fryer and bring it to 380 F. In a bowl, beat the egg and buttermilk. On a plate, combine breadcrumbs, salt, and pepper. Dip each finger into the egg mixture, roll it up in the crumbs, and spritz it with cooking spray. Arrange on the greased frying basket and AirFry for 10 minutes, turning once. Serve with aioli.

Crispy Haddock Cake

INGREDIENTS (2 Servings)

8 oz haddock, cooked and flaked

2 potatoes, cooked and mashed

2 tbsp green olives, pitted and chopped

1 tbsp fresh cilantro, chopped

1 tsp lemon zest

1 egg, beaten

DIRECTIONS (Total Time: 25 minutes + refrigerating time)

Mix haddock, lemon zest, olives, cilantro, egg, and potatoes. Shape into patties and chill for 60 minutes. Turn on the air fryer and bring it to 350 F. Place the patties in the greased frying basket and AirFry for 12-14 minutes, flipping once, halfway through cooking until golden. Serve with green salad or steamed rice.

Seafood Casserole with Cheddar Cheese and Red Chili

INGREDIENTS (4 Servings)

1 cup seafood mix

1 lb russet potatoes, peeled and quartered

1 carrot, grated

½ fennel bulb, sliced

2 tbsp fresh parsley, chopped

10 oz baby spinach

1 small tomato, diced

½ celery stick, grated

2 tbsp butter

4 tbsp milk

½ cup cheddar cheese, grated

1 small red chili, minced

Salt and black pepper to taste

DIRECTIONS (Total Time: 60 minutes + cooling time)

Cover the potatoes with salted water in a pot and cook over medium heat for 18-20 minutes or until tender. Drain and mash them along with butter, milk, salt, and pepper. Mix until smooth and set aside. In a bowl, mix celery, carrot, red chili, fennel, parsley, seafood mix, tomato, spinach, salt, and pepper. Turn on the air fryer and bring it to 330 F. In a casserole baking dish, spread the seafood mixture. Top with the potato mash and level. Sprinkle with cheddar cheese and place the dish in the air fryer. Bake for 20-25 minutes or until golden and bubbling at the edges. Let cool for 10 minutes, slice, and serve.

Creole Trout Fillets

INGREDIENTS (4 Servings)

4 skin-on trout fillets

2 tsp creole seasoning

2 tbsp fresh dill, chopped

1 lemon, sliced

DIRECTIONS (Total Time: 20 minutes)

Turn on the air fryer and bring it to 350 F. Season the trout with creole seasoning on both sides and spray with cooking spray. Place in the frying basket and Bake for 10-12 minutes, flipping once. Serve sprinkled with dill and garnished with lemon slices.

Salmon Fillets

INGREDIENTS (2 Servings)

2 salmon fillets

1 tbsp olive oil Salt to taste

1 lemon, cut into wedges

DIRECTIONS (Total Time: 15 minutes)

Turn on the air fryer and bring it to 380 F. Brush the salmon with olive oil and season with salt. Place the fillets in the greased frying basket and Bake for 8 minutes until tender, turning once. Serve with lemon wedges.

Salmon with Greek Sauce

INGREDIENTS (4 Servings)

1 lb salmon fillets

Salt and black pepper to taste

2 tsp olive oil

2 tbsp fresh dill, chopped

1 cup sour cream

1 cup Greek yogurt

DIRECTIONS (Total Time: 20 minutes)

In a bowl, mix the sour cream, Greek yogurt, dill, and salt. Keep in the fridge until ready to use. Turn on the air fryer and bring it to 340 F. Drizzle the fillets with olive oil and sprinkle with salt and pepper. Place the fish in the frying basket and Bake for 10-12 minutes, flipping once. Serve drizzled with the Greek sauce.

Tuna Patties

INGREDIENTS (2 Servings)

5 oz canned tuna

1 tsp lime juice

½ tsp paprika

¼ cup flour

½ cup milk

1 small onion, diced

2 eggs

1 tsp chili powder, optional

½ tsp salt

DIRECTIONS (Total Time: 25 minutes + refrigerating time)
Place all ingredients   in a bowl and mix well. Make two large patties
out of the mixture. Refrigerate them for 30 minutes. Then, remove and
AirFry the patties in the greased frying basket for 13-15 minutes at 350
F, flipping once halfway through cooking. Serve warm.

French Trout a la Meunière

INGREDIENTS (4 Servings)

4 trout pieces

½ cup flour

Salt to taste

2 tbsp butter

1 lemon, juiced

2 tbsp chervil (French parsley), chopped

DIRECTIONS (Total Time: 20 minutes)

Turn on the air fryer and bring it to 380 F. Season the trout with salt and dredge in the flour. Spritz with cooking oil and AirFry for 12-14 minutes, flipping once, until crispy. Remove and tent with foil to keep warm. Melt the butter in a skillet over medium heat. Stir for 1-2 minutes until the butter becomes golden brown. Turn off the heat and stir in chervil and lemon juice. Pour the sauce over the fish and serve.

Fried Catfish

INGREDIENTS (2 Servings)

4 catfish fillets, cut into strips

½ cup polenta ½ cup flour

¼ tsp cayenne pepper

1 tbsp fresh parsley, chopped

Salt and black pepper to taste

1 tsp onion powder

1 (7-oz) bottle club soda

1 lemon, sliced

DIRECTIONS (Total Time: 25 minutes)

Preheat the fryer to 400 F. Sift the flour into a large bowl. Add in the onion powder, salt, black pepper, and cayenne pepper and stir to combine. Pour in the soda and whisk until a smooth batter is formed. Lightly spray the fish with cooking spray. Dip the fish strips into the batter, then into the polenta. Put the fillets in the lightly greased frying basket and AirFry for 6-7 minutes. Flip or shake and cook further for 4-5 minutes or until brown and crispy. Garnish with parsley and lemon slices and serve.

Cod Fillets

INGREDIENTS (4 Servings)

1 cup breadcrumbs

2 tbsp olive oil

2 eggs, beaten

4 cod fillets

A pinch of salt

1 cup flour

DIRECTIONS (Total Time: 20 minutes)

Turn on the air fryer and bring it to 390 F. Mix the crumbs, olive oil, and salt in a bowl. In another bowl, beat the eggs. Put the flour into a third bowl. Toss the cod fillets in the flour, then in the eggs, and finally in the crumbs mixture. Place them in the greased frying basket and AirFry for 10 minutes. At the 6-minute mark, quickly turn the fillets. Remove to a plate and serve with dill-yogurt sauce if desired.

Black Cod with Fennel and Pecans

INGREDIENTS (2 Servings)

2 black cod fillets

Salt and black pepper to taste

1 small fennel bulb, sliced

½ cup pecans

2 tsp white balsamic vinegar

2 tbsp olive oil

DIRECTIONS (Total Time: 25 minutes)

Turn on the air fryer and bring it to 400 F. Season the fillets with salt and pepper and drizzle with some olive oil. Place in them the frying basket and AirFry for 10-12 minutes, flipping once, or until golden brown. Meanwhile, warm the remaining olive oil in a skillet over medium heat. Stir-fry the fennel for 5 minutes. Add in the pecans and cook for 3-4 minutes until toasted. Drizzle with the balsamic vinegar and season with salt and pepper. Stir well and remove from heat. Pour the mixture over the black cod and serve.

Spicy Sardine Cake

INGREDIENTS (4 Servings)

2 (4-oz) tins sardines, chopped

2 eggs, beaten

½ cup breadcrumbs

⅓ cup green onions, finely chopped

2 tbsp fresh parsley, chopped

1 tbsp mayonnaise

1 tsp sweet chili sauce

½ tsp paprika

Salt and black pepper to taste

2 tbsp olive oil

DIRECTIONS (Total Time: 20 minutes)

In a bowl, add sardines, eggs, breadcrumbs, green onions, parsley, mayonnaise, sweet chili sauce, paprika, salt, and black pepper. Mix well with hands. Shape into 8 cakes and brush them lightly with olive oil. AirFry them for 8-10 minutes at 390 F, flipping once halfway through cooking. Serve warm.

White Fish Fillets with Romano Cheese

INGREDIENTS (4 Servings)

2 tbsp fresh basil, chopped

1 tsp garlic powder

2 tbsp Romano cheese, grated

Salt and black pepper to taste

4 white fish fillets

DIRECTIONS (Total Time: 20 minutes)

Turn on the air fryer and bring it to 350 F. Season fillets with garlic, salt, and pepper. Place them in the greased frying basket and AirFry for 8-10 minutes, flipping once. Serve topped with Romano cheese and basil.

Jamaican Hoki Fillets

INGREDIENTS (4 Servings)

4 hoki fillets

1 tbsp ground Jamaican allspice

1 tsp paprika

Salt and garlic powder to taste

½ red onion, sliced

2 tomatoes, chopped

½ cup canned corn, drained

½ lemon, juiced

DIRECTIONS (Total Time: 20 minutes)

In a bowl, mix the red onion, tomatoes, corn, salt, and lemon juice; toss to coat and set aside. Turn on the air fryer and bring it to 390 F. In a bowl, mix paprika, garlic powder, and Jamaican seasoning. Rub the hoki fillets with the spices mixture. Spritz with cooking spray. Transfer to the frying basket and AirFry for 8 minutes, turn the fillets, and cook further for 5 minutes or until crispy. Serve with the corn salsa.

Kimchi Salmon

INGREDIENTS (4 Servings)

2 tbsp soy sauce

2 tbsp sesame oil

2 tbsp mirin

1 tbsp ginger puree

1 tsp kimchi spice

1 tsp sriracha sauce

2 lb salmon fillets

1 lime, cut into wedges

DIRECTIONS (Total Time: 20 minutes)

Turn on the air fryer and bring it to 350 F. Grease the frying basket with cooking spray. In a bowl, mix together soy sauce, mirin, ginger puree, kimchi spice, and sriracha sauce. Add the salmon and toss to coat. Place the fillets in the frying basket and drizzle with sesame oil. Bake for 10-12 minutes, flipping once halfway through. Garnish with lime wedges and serve.

FOTO 2

"Blackened" Catfish

INGREDIENTS (2 Servings)

2 catfish fillets

2 tsp blackening seasoning

Juice of 1 lime

2 tbsp butter, melted

1 garlic clove, minced

2 tbsp fresh cilantro, chopped

DIRECTIONS (Total Time: 25 minutes)

Turn on the air fryer and bring it to 360 F. In a bowl, mix garlic, lime juice, cilantro, and butter. Divide the sauce into two parts, rub 1 part of the sauce onto the fillets. Sprinkle with the seasoning. Place the fillets in the greased frying basket and Bake for 14-16 minutes, flipping once. Serve with the remaining sauce.

Oaty Salmon and Haddock Fishcake

INGREDIENTS   (4 Servings)

4 potatoes, cooked and mashed

2 salmon fillets, cubed

1 haddock fillet, cubed

1 tsp Dijon mustard

½ cup oats

2 tbsp fresh dill, chopped

2 tbsp olive oil

Salt and black pepper to taste

DIRECTIONS (Total Time: 30 minutes)

Turn on the air fryer and bring it to 400 F. Boil salmon and haddock cubes in a pot filled with salted water over medium heat, for 5-8 minutes. Drain, cool, and pat dry. Flake or shred the fish and transfer to a bowl. Let cool slightly and mix in the mashed potatoes, mustard, oats, dill, salt, and black pepper. Shape into balls and flatten to make patties. Brush with olive oil and arrange them in the greased frying basket. Bake for 10-13 minutes, flipping once halfway through, until golden. Let cool slightly before serving.

Parmesan Cheese Fillets

INGREDIENTS (4 Servings)

¾ cup Parmesan cheese, grated

2 tbsp olive oil

2 tsp paprika

2 tbsp fresh parsley, chopped

¼ tsp garlic powder

4 tilapia fillets

DIRECTIONS (Total Time: 20 minutes)

Turn on the air fryer and bring it to 350 F. Mix parsley, Parmesan cheese, garlic powder, and paprika in a shallow bowl. Coat fillets in the mixture and brush with olive oil. Place the filets in the frying basket and AirFry for 10-12 minutes, flipping once, until golden brown. Serve immediately.

Corn Tortillas with Halibut Fillets

INGREDIENTS (4 Servings)

4 corn tortillas

1 lb halibut fillets, sliced into strips

2 tbsp olive oil

1 ½ cups flour

1 (12-oz) can beer

A pinch of salt

4 tbsp peach salsa

4 tsp fresh cilantro, chopped

1 tsp baking powder

DIRECTIONS (Total Time: 25 minutes)

Preheat the fryer to 390 F. In a bowl, mix flour, baking powder, and salt. Pour in 1-2 oz of beer, enough to form a batter-like consistency. Save the rest of the beer to gulp with the tacos. Dip the fish strips into the beer batter. Arrange them in the greased frying basket and AirFry them for 8-10 minutes, shaking or flipping once. Spread the peach salsa on the tortillas. Serve topped with the strips and cilantro.

Lemon Pepper Haddock

INGREDIENTS (4 Servings)

4 haddock fillets

1 cup breadcrumbs

2 tbsp lemon juice

Salt and black pepper to taste

~ 74 ~

¼ cup potato flakes

2 eggs, beaten

¼ cup Parmesan cheese, grated

3 tbsp flour

DIRECTIONS (Total Time: 20 minutes)

In a bowl, combine flour, salt, and pepper. In another bowl, mix breadcrumbs, Parmesan, and potato flakes. Dip fillets in the flour first, then in the eggs, and coat them in the crumbs mixture. Place them in the greased frying basket and AirFry for 14-16 minutes at 370 F, flipping once. Serve with lemon juice.

FOTO 3

Pistachio Crusted Salmon

INGREDIENTS (2 Servings)

2 salmon fillets

1 tsp yellow mustard

4 tbsp pistachios, chopped

Salt and black pepper to taste

1 tsp garlic powder

2 tsp lemon juice

2 tbsp Parmesan cheese, grated

1 tsp olive oil

DIRECTIONS (Total Time: 25 minutes)

Turn on the air fryer and bring it to 350 F. Whisk together the mustard, olive oil, lemon juice, salt, black pepper, and garlic powder in a bowl. Rub the mustard mixture evenly onto the salmon fillets. Lay the fillets on the greased frying basket, skin side down and spread the pistachios and Parmesan cheese all over; press down gently to make a crust. Bake the salmon for 12-15 minutes until golden.

Marinated Tuna with Red Pepper Flakes

INGREDIENTS (4 Servings)

4 tuna steaks

1 cup Japanese ponzu sauce

2 tbsp sesame oil

1 tbsp red pepper flakes

2 tbsp ginger paste

¼ cup scallions, sliced

Salt and black pepper to taste

DIRECTIONS (Total Time: 25 minutes + marinating time)

In a bowl, mix the ponzu sauce, sesame oil, red pepper flakes, ginger paste, salt, and black pepper. Add in the tuna and toss to coat. Cover and marinate for 60 minutes in the fridge. Turn on the air fryer and bring it to 380 F. Remove tuna from the marinade and arrange the steaks on the greased frying basket. AirFry for 14-16 minutes, turning once. Top with scallions and serve with fresh salad.

Cod Fingers

INGREDIENTS (4 Servings)

2 cups flour

Salt and black pepper to taste

1 tsp seafood seasoning

1 cup cornmeal

1 lb cod fillets, cut into fingers

2 tbsp milk

2 eggs, beaten

1 cup breadcrumbs

DIRECTIONS (Total Time: 20 minutes)

Turn on the air fryer and bring it to 400 F. In a bowl, mix the eggs with milk, salt, and black pepper. In a separate bowl, mix the flour, cornmeal, and seafood seasoning. In a third bowl, pour the breadcrumbs. Roll the cod fingers in the flour mixture, then dip in the egg mixture, and finally coat with the breadcrumbs. Place the fingers in the frying basket and AirFry for 12-14 minutes, shaking once or twice. Serve hot.

Catfish Fillets

INGREDIENTS (4 Servings)

4 catfish fillets

¼ cup seasoned fish fry

1 tbsp olive oil

1 tbsp fresh rosemary, chopped

DIRECTIONS (Total Time: 20 minutes)

Turn on the air fryer and bring it to 400 F. Add the seasoned fish fry and the fillets to a large Ziploc bag; massage to coat. Place the fillets in the greased frying basket and AirFry for 6-8 minutes. Flip the fillets and cook for 2-4 more minutes or until golden and crispy. Top with freshly chopped rosemary and serve.

Salmon and Onion Balls

INGREDIENTS (2 Servings)

1 cup tinned salmon

¼ celery stalk, chopped

1 spring onion, sliced

4 tbsp wheat germ

2 tbsp olive oil

1 large egg

1 tbsp fresh dill, chopped

½ tsp garlic powder

DIRECTIONS (Total Time: 20 minutes)

Turn on the air fryer and bring it to 390 F. In a large bowl, mix tinned salmon, egg, celery, onion, dill, and garlic. Shape the mixture into balls and roll them up in wheat germ. Carefully flatten and place them in the greased frying basket. AirFry for 8-10 minutes, flipping once halfway through, or until golden.

FOTO 4

Salmon Cake with Fresh Parsley

INGREDIENTS (4 Servings)

12 oz cooked salmon

2 potatoes, boiled and mashed

½ cup flour

2 tbsp capers, chopped

2 tbsp fresh parsley, chopped

1 tbsp olive oil

Zest of 1 lemon

DIRECTIONS (Total Time: 25 minutes + marinating time)
Place the mashed potatoes in a bowl and flake the salmon over. Stir in capers, parsley, and lemon zest. Mix well and shape into 4 cakes. Roll them up in flour, shake off, and refrigerate for 1 hour. Turn on the air fryer and bring it to 350 F. Remove the cakes and brush them with olive oil. Bake in the greased frying basket for 12-14 minutes, flipping once halfway through cooking. Serve warm.

Salmon Croquettes with mayonnaise

INGREDIENTS   (4 Servings)

1 (15 oz) tinned salmon, flaked

1 cup onions, grated

1 cup carrots, grated

3 large eggs

1 ½ tbsp fresh chives, chopped

4 tbsp mayonnaise 4 tbsp breadcrumbs

2 ½ tsp Italian seasoning

Salt and black pepper to taste

2 ½ tsp lemon juice

DIRECTIONS (Total Time: 20 minutes + refrigerating time)

In a bowl, mix well the salmon, onions, carrots, eggs, chives, mayonnaise, crumbs, Italian seasoning, salt, black pepper, and lemon juice. Form croquettes out of the mixture and refrigerate for 45 minutes. Turn on the air fryer and bring it to 400 F. Grease the basket with cooking spray. Arrange the croquettes in a single layer and spray with cooking spray. AirFry for 10-12 minutes until golden, flipping once.

Salmon Fillets with Broccoli

INGREDIENTS (2 Servings)

2 salmon fillets

2 tsp olive oil

Juice of 1 lime

1 tsp red chili flakes (optional)

Salt and black pepper to taste

5 oz broccoli florets, steamed

DIRECTIONS (Total Time: 25 minutes)

In a bowl, add 1 tbsp of olive oil, lime juice, salt, and pepper and rub the mixture onto the fillets. Transfer to them to the frying basket. Drizzle the florets with the remaining olive oil and arrange them around the salmon. Bake in the preheated at 340 F air fryer for 14 minutes or until the salmon is fork-tender and crispy on top. Sprinkle the fillets with red chili flakes (optional) and serve with broccoli.

MEASUREMENT

CONVERSIONS

WEIGHT EQUIVALENTS

US STANDARD	METRIC (APPROXIMATE)
½ OUNCE	15 GRAMS
1 OUNCE	30 GRAMS
2 OUNCES	60 GRAMS
4 OUNCES	115 GRAMS
8 OUNCES	225 GRAMS
12 OUNCES	340 GRAMS
16 OUNCES OR 1 POUND	455 GRAMS

VOLUME EQUIVALENTS (DRY)

US STANDARD	METRIC (APPROXIMATE)
¼ TEASPOON	1 ML
½ TEASPOON	2 ML
1 TEASPOON	4 ML
1 TABLESPOON	15 ML
¼ CUP	59 ML
½ CUP	118 ML
¾ CUP	177 ML
1 CUP	235 ML

VOLUME EQUIVALENTS (LIQUID)

US STANDARD	METRIC (APPROXIMATE)
2 TABLESPOONS	30 ML
¼ CUP	60 ML
½ CUP	240 ML
2 CUPS	475 ML

AIR FRYER TEMPERATURES

FAHRENHEIT (F)	CELSIUS (APPROXIMATE)
250°F	120°C
300°F	150°C
325°F	165°C
350°F	180°C
375°F	190°C
400°F	200°C
425°F	220°C

AIR FRYER COOKING CHART

FISH AND SEAFOOD					
ITEM	TEMP (°F)	TIME (MINS)	ITEM	TEMP (°F)	TIME (MINS)
FISH FILLET (8 OZ)	400	10-12	CALAMARI (8 OZ)	400	4-10
SALMON FILLET (8 OZ)	300	12-14	SCALLOPS (1 LB)	400	5-8
TUNA STEAK (6 OZ)	400	7-10	SHRIMP (1 LB)	3900	5-8

CREDITS

https://pixabay.com/

www.pexels.com

unsplash.com

www.Bing.com

FOTO 1 "fresh fish n chips" by f10n4 is licensed under CC BY 2.0FOTO 2 "luz ribs" by goodiesfirst is licensed under CC BY 2.0

FOTO 2 "Blackened Catfish" by HarshLight is licensed under CC BY 2.0

FOTO 3 Alex Cooks CC-BY-SA

FOTO 4 – FREE IMAGES CC

CPSIA information can be obtained
at www.ICGtesting.com
Printed in the USA
BVHW091928230621
610293BV00008B/1156